M000116603

The Poet & The Architect

Also by Christine Stewart-Nuñez

Bluewords Greening
Untrussed
Keeping Them Alive
Postcard on Parchment

Edited
South Dakota in Poems
Scholars and Poets Talk About Queens
Action, Influence, Voice: Contemporary South Dakota Women

The Poet & The Architect

Christine Stewart-Nuñez

Terrapin Books

© 2021 by Christine Stewart-Nuñez
Printed in the United States of America.
All rights reserved.
No part of this book may be reproduced in any manner,
except for brief quotations embodied in critical articles
or reviews.

Terrapin Books
4 Midvale Avenue
West Caldwell, NJ 07006

www.terrapinbooks.com

ISBN: 978-1-947896-45-1
Library of Congress Control Number: 2021936794

First Edition

Cover art by Brian T. Rex

To Brian, life-builder extraordinaire,
and my boys, Holden and Xavier

Contents

🌀   Ring Four

An architect, to be a true exponent of his time, must possess first, last and always the sympathy, the intuition of a poet...
—Louis Sullivan

Ring One

Poet Prepares for Love

[B]eing more abstract allowed me to express the essence of things rather than reproducing what I saw.
—Ruth Leaf

Peony:
Bashfulness hides
in the knot, in pearl-white
petals trimmed red. The spring blossom's
stamens
are velvet threads, bunched and centered,
a goldenrod tassel
gathered in wait
for wind.

Nosegay:
Flowers clutch—leaf
to leaf, ruby bloom to
ruby bloom—this traditional
tango
bouquet where stems brush as if thighs
pressed in a cross-stepped
walk, in a closed
embrace.

A mix
in *Amity*:
Stems of meadow grasses
and wildflowers, heavy with
sun, arc
as if breeze-blown, and here they thrive
with leaves intertwined. They
touch in summer's
full flush.

Architect Annotates the Margins

Youngstown was taken
down. Detroit is falling.
That's tectonicide.

To a designer, the only thing
more uselessly beautiful than
construction is destruction.

I've had enough dark
sky in my rear-view mirror.

In a Past Life, We Met at the Cataract Hotel

Derby tilted, triangle of necktie
visible above his coat, he slid
over and set down a sketchbook. I
glimpsed the corner of a grid
inked over, but it was his hands
I'd recognize a century later,
the way they rendered scans
of places that intrigued him. The waiter
served gin cocktails and he mused
aloud urban ideas for that new city
and I listened and wondered, confused
by my own life but in love with pretty
words and drawings and connection—
a longing sparked by his attention.

Congruence

I'm caught by Allan D'Arcangelo's
Web, a painting of a sculpture's maroon

and rust-red beams which bleed
off the canvas, its crisscross intersections

creating triangles—vibrant blue—
the color of my lover's favorite pants,

and so I write *Web* into a building,
declaim a ledge and roof and simple

geometries since I can strip rectangles
and squares from the canvas until

it becomes our bed and a beam his torso
swathed in sheets, legs sticking over

the side, and if he saw *Web,* he'd argue
tone, the saturation difference of orange

and neon orange, he'd say, Take art
for what it says, but don't always believe.

Close-up, I study buildings by their bones
and joints, not their silhouettes;

close-up, his scent, sound, and skin
persuade me: come, come closer, come.

Dimensional Shift

His hands sketch walls
that renounce boundaries
when he draws me in.

I saw squares, lines locked
into height and width until
he said cylinder, cube.

How grids blurred: the scent
of his neck's slope, the void
between our clutched palms.

Space cracked open
my mind's eye, a chick's
sharp beak emerging.

To taste place, the juice
of stone, I meet his green
eyes and whisper   hips.

This is how he builds me:
patterned blocks of words
turn arc into umbrella.

Didactic

Love is an intense form of curiosity.
—Monica Barron

Throw open the library
of your body. Run
your fingertips across

this shelf's spine, over
atlases, dictionaries,
novels. Your hands—

wide, strong—are lenses
that ignite encyclopedic
knowledge; let's burn

in biography, biology.
Ask questions. Unlock
the map of scars, read

lines of ribs, linger
at the hip, memorize
the archives' lips.

Stretch your supple
pages until you are open—
explicit and known.

The Poetry Foundation

Does he recall the first words he offered,
sentences tossed across the blank page?

William Carlos Williams. I missed his
pass but felt the tug of contact—hook

set, line invisible. The second time
Brown's thing theory landed in my lap

for analysis. Our missives, written across
midnights and sunrises, sent across town,

across time, across country (can you see
this map?) reveal poché: space drawn

by the contrails of fingertips. Then
there were spirals: land art, garden art,

bike path graffiti. We spoke the same
language with different alphabets.

He knew he'd marry me when he saw
my books at the Poetry Foundation.

He arrived for the building;
he left with me, bona fide.

Theft

For this I've looted his letters—
this heart-print, this syllable-quilt—
pillaging photos and lyrics
and text to trace love: I like loops;

your loops are even more lovely.
For gems I've looted his letters,
skimming sentences with my hand,
squashing sound in my clutch:

I dipped and circled you in theory,
no body of work to build on.
For wit I've looted his letters,
for parallels: Architecture

works in stories, and you pulled me
off my axis. I cut out swaths
of words to plat our origin.
For love I've looted his letters.

An Architect's Kiss

The night before a technician
x-rays angles of my breast

because the doctor felt a fullness
(one I can't find though I've probed)

my husband takes both in his hands.
Years ago, a physician aspirated

a plugged milk duct, the nugget
reappearing the next day. Just

the architecture of your breast,
she'd said. Not an architect

of muscle, fat, skin, or bone,
my husband still imagines interiors

in these dense palmfuls, and he
considers knots inside this beaded

physiology, duct-rooms within these
castles of cells. Before he brushes

my lips, he holds my breasts
with sinewy fingers, kissing them

as if spheres of blown glass, again—
again. He attends, my body blessed.

Love on a Grid

we grasp
flat surfaces

like spreadsheet cells,
one a bed

taut space stretching
end to end

an emptiness like
a countertop

scrubbed clean
or a calendar

turned, new
month ready

or a desk
marked

with stray dashes
and ink stains

sheet of white
paper beckoning

He Said, She Said

He said algebra.
She said alchemy.

He said lines, quadrilaterals, parallelograms, dodecagons.
She said curve.

He said, I'm on cigarette time.
She said, I borrow it from sleep.

He said, It's all angles and spirals.
She said, Open up that space right now.

He said, orange and black and white.
She said, cerulean, cardinal, turquoise, lime.

He said grid, list, distance.
She said bridal, fire, wild.

He said, I dream and wake up.
She said, I dream flesh and gold.

He said pattern, project.
She said pussycat and pastel and pink.

He said, Watch how I dot this point.
She said, Even my shadows are bold.

He said, Let me fall into this maze, this detail, this cohesion of color.
She said, Don't let me fall.

All My Engineering

I want to engineer
us, so I sketch black lines
on a future's blueprint, form
squares with my fingers, press
words into an art-deco-cubist-

Frank-Lloyd-Wright something.
Structures quicken my heart.
If only relationship building
meant five-hour What If sessions
surfing possibilities, library

books spilling out of my bag,
magazines coffee-stained, your
shadow over me at the keyboard.
I overlook buckets of paint, piles
of sawdust, hammers cracking

new headaches; it's the stories
we'll write with that bedroom,
this bathroom. When I lose
the signals, I want to engineer us.
The mechanics of machine

and microchip, the ways electrons
scoot across a circuit of silicon,
should account for failure.
The math of transistors and logic
gates should predict what happens

when your answers resolve
to unstable processes, refrains
of not enough: bandwidth, will,
patience. I want to engineer us,
which can mean carry out through

artful contrivance, but I just want
to manage the flow of data—
make it grounded and free
after all these testing years.

Ring Two

Outlaw

I've stared at ceilings, popcorned, orange-
peeled, water stained. On my tour
of brothels, Deadwood's last one closing
in the 1980s, I photographed museums
of wallpaper, their peeling layers: dulled
colors and textures covered with pastel
stripes or florals. These were much seen
ceilings, someone said. I couldn't watch

Deadwood because sex on screens devoid
of love and desire—at least for one—
turns me off. I'm not opposed to women
being paid for sex, just how desperation
drives the exchange. Even Calamity Jane—
cook, waitress, scout, and dance-hall girl
of the Wild West—worked this way as need
demanded. I studied her tombstone on my visit.
She's buried next to Wild Bill Hickok,
and I passed the saloon where he was shot
playing poker. Gambling's a permitted vice,
prostitution's illegal. Technically.

Who isn't desperate from time to time?
I've opened for love and not desire,
and I've opened for desire and not love.
Once in a Deadwood hotel, my knee-high
boots and leather jacket peeled off,
I poured myself into a man I'd just met,
poured myself into the gaping hole
divorce left. Outlaws don't care what bonds

sex severs. In the Wild West, anyone's
touch could summon me, the past
papered over—no questions asked.

Cleave

my hand on the middle of his back his cheek against mine
I know texture and tone his pleasure like my own now
and I track waves until a memory breaks until the moment is rent in two
he no longer hears her words those viruses have insinuated themselves
they're hard-wired, chimeras too late for inoculation
tongue and touch are eradication's tools each stolen hour, each midnight minute

Palimpsest

We lean on the bridge's bones, spine of rust, ruins
of iron, a picture of life against ruins.

Abandoned means maples, oaks, and cedars are free
to touch your forehead and say: New love, trust ruins.

An arch of stone and an arch of *I do* span walls,
St. Anthony Falls, two lives, and a park's ruins.

Abandoned is the heel's impression as the foot
steps away, a mark smoothed when we discussed ruins.

Before we met, you called out to me. When the words
arrived in my ear, I thought they were just ruins.

At the shell of a river mill, ghost flour falls
through the air; flakes of factory snow dust ruins.

My love, the landscape subsumed my past and yours
and left a trace upon which our vows trussed ruins.

Medical Arts Building, Watertown

Like a
second-time bride,
she wears white well even
if self-conscious—porcelain tiles
dimpled.
Still, adorned with understated
ornament in the midst
of rough and bulk,
she shines.

Brand: Bring Your Dreams

—Brookings, South Dakota

bring your dreams that need four full seasons
bring your dreams that need a hunter's moon
bring your dreams that need August's humid heat
bring your dreams that need June floods
bring your dreams that need the ice of March and artic winds in April
bring your dreams that need space and seed them across the prairie
bring your dreams

bring your dreams that wear jeans on Sunday
bring your dreams that eat beef
bring your dreams that sing karaoke
bring your dreams that draw midnight couples home
brings your dreams that require blisters and study blitzes
bring your dreams that crack open at sunrise
bring your dreams

don't bring dreams that break The Rules
don't bring fancy or flighty or phenomenal
don't bring too smart or too sharp or too sexy
don't bring the stink of city
don't bring wacky or wasteful
don't bring champagne—beer's king here

if your dreams wear sequins, cover with a cardigan
if your dreams speak with an accent, everyone will notice
if your dreams savor the spicy, supply your own hot sauce
if your dreams critique the status quo, speak them slant
even if your dreams were already here, still bring them

bring your dreams and spring them loose from doubt
bring your dreams and string them together from scraps
bring your dreams and sixty hours a week
bring your dreams and fail at perfection
bring your dreams and sleep on them
bring your dreams

she brings dreams of cyclones and sex
she brings dreams of cliff-diving and chislic
she brings dreams of roots and rhymes and riots
she brings dreams of silence
she brings dreams and a broken heart, empty wallet, new baby

he brings dreams of baseball and bonanzas and brews
he brings dreams of one more try for love
he brings dreams of catfish and kayaks
he brings dreams of peace
he brings dreams blessed by snowflakes and seawater

bring your dreams to connect with spirit
bring your dreams to build shelter
bring your dreams to weave with another's
bring your dreams to reinvent yourself
bring your dreams to create a fine life

Witch Loves Architect

My husband writes shelter; I architect spells.
Word-building bridges graphics and sites
to make place. With cauldron models,
my husband writes shelter. I architect spells
by conjuring lines my hand compels.
Casting material insights,
my husband writes shelter. I architect spells:
word-building bridges graphics and sites.

Remodel

When our love was new, each night we locked
long and steady. You drew me in with a strong
hand like the blue-lined arcs you'd fanned
across paper. Passion no longer shocked
you. And now, nineteen weeks along
and my body under renovation, I stand
here, waiting. Let practice return your touch
to a new draft, my reset body. Pull
me close. Iterations will appear
if you trust the process. You perceive such
details intuitively and know what full
projects can be. Not me. More than the fear
you won't need to hold me? That I'll withhold
my own desire until it's grown cold.

Negative Space

His side of the bed
is a wide expanse

of sand smoothed
by waves. My fingers

and toes stretch
into coolness—

a moment of sleepy
desire—expecting

heat, expecting
skin. Absence

jolts my spleen.
Where he's wandered,

where he sleeps
I only guess.

Couch, office
floor, deck chaises

seduce. I
imagine what

anchors him,
and the breeze-

stirred trees remind:
not me, not me.

When You're Away, I Consider Form

I don't make any separations. A poem is a poem.
A building's a building.... I mean, it's all structure.
　　　　　　　　　—John Hejduk

I need villanelles of you pulling
my breath like lines moving down

the page and the promise of rhyme
bending my ear. I need a sestina

of touch, patterns of palm, stroke,
skim, brush, and rub returning—

a cycle of sound and pressure I
apprehend in my bones. I need

the triolet's refrain rolling off
your tongue like a sample, new

and nuanced here and here and here.
It's all structure is why I need angles

of play, the love our bodies build.
I miss you. The ache's more sour

than a dropped foot, a forced rhyme.
If you're free from me too long,

what will you jettison first? Meter?
Lines? Come home. Our sonnet's

the fourteen creases in the sheets.
A couplet of light greens your eyes

only inches from mine when iambs
ascend atop iambs. Please. I need

you in haiku: distilled in syllables,
laid bare in the last line's turn.

The Process of an Architect's Thinking

1.

Agitation. One question's sharp edge
against another's point and his pencil
tip quivers; the splice and connection
of curiosity spin ideas until, dizzy,
he attends. Design moves beyond
décor—a shell with meaning's meat
scooped out. Architecture sends tendrils
into sleep, songs, supper, sex. Images
ignite facts. Everything vibrates with
possibility, answers emerging from
iterations made in midnight's cradle.
Before serendipity shows up. Before
conversations act as catalysts. Here
he is, fingers spread over paper,
teasing a thread from the knot.

2.

Translation. The idea's shape is distilled
from his neocortex by a pixel riot,
by a cultivation of context. It spills forth
from a phrase spoken just so, sketched
through friction, a strand of ink rolling
out while the hand defines rhythm.
Translation's a ream of paper, a document
list, software frozen, the neighborhood's
sole glowing light at 3 a.m., wine stain
on the drafting table. Discovery's revealed
in slippage, the surprise between lines
and drafts, the recollection of precedent

like an old friend's laughter summoned
by song. Before the final images crystallize,
before sleep clears the slate, the screen's
light illumines his furrowed brow.

   3.
Articulation. Not a sound stutter but
an idea all zipped up. Walls mean with lines,
angles, corners. Balance and harmony
he perceives in a glance, a holistic
moment of alignment. When articulate,
the structure sings. In the body's
line of logic, articulation's a joint
between bones. In botany, a juncture.
In my language, the right word
in the right place at the right time.
Joint, juncture, precision—he looks
and looks and looks again at different
times and angles. He crosses every t,
dots every i—nothing's an inch off
or a material ill-fitted. Articulation's
deliberate and recursive, process
and product beyond *good enough*.
Before print is pressed, before an idea
is pushed, his face registers articulation:
he blinks and looks away.

   4.
Submission. He lets go of his grip,
he lets edges recede, his fingertips retract
from the model, paper, keyboard. He gives
up so he can give into, let someone else
take in the project whole, his idea-made-
material coursing through their minds.

An encounter: this critique, this review.
Trust built in, he surrenders ego—or
wishes to, intends to. Doesn't everyone?
He flinches. He folds his arms, cocks
his head, looks askew. He argues. He
defends. Submission makes the drawing
loosen, geometries melting or exploding,
volume wrestled to the ground. But he sees
possibility, new iterations with potential.
He sighs. He smiles. He persists.

Intuition Assay

Our story isn't one of love at first sight.
Our introduction felt the way a puzzle piece,
finally placed, reveals an image—direct
sensory apprehension. In a crowd, I heard

his name and I knew his silhouette,
the grammar of his shape. He hoped
to elope to a town unknown to me:
Owatonna, Minnesota, and marry

in Sullivan's jewel-box bank. Painted cows
in pastures peered down on the queue
and my skin felt like church from the stained-
glass sunlight. The bank refused us,

but I understood: for him, tying the knot
in that Wells Fargo meant art's blessing.
With my poet's sympathy, it meant
the setting for a marriage of history

and imagination—a deliberate design.
Knowing without reason felt romantic,
like faith. But brain experts say intuition
is really experience, precedent. It's why he,

with his Bauhaus cubes, with his naked
swatches of color, with his preference for
clean and bold, praised the jewel-box's brick
and green terra cotta bands, its cast iron

electroliers, its president's corner office—
rooms for a bank's every need. His whispers
of awe and explanation ascended:
geometrical precision inside and out.

When I saw Sullivan's name on a radiator
screen at the Art Institute of Chicago,
I recognized patterns, material. Steel lace:
overlapping parabolas of spirals, dots, curls.

I imagined a lace-making strategy: one-
thousand intricacies in play as pins
are placed, as bobbins are spun and coded.
For the screen, Sullivan drew out the lace

on paper sheaths and ordered them cast.
I wondered if Sullivan studied his mother's
lace linens, the trim of skirts and bodices.
I wondered if those patterns felt as intuitive

to him as my husband is to me. I can't see
versions of me in his past; rather, gaps—
what cuts left my shape. Perhaps that's why
the perfect wedding spot was outside where

steel, stone, and water intersected a city's
center, a place we'd both seen the day before
and said *here*. Intuition. It seems we've
internalized taste on different paths

and landed here, holding hands before
a radiator screen, our son asleep in his stroller
as we breathe in the quiet space, mesmerized
by curls and arcs and spheres of steel.

Urban Planning

*The project of Lead, South Dakota is to negotiate between the
Homestake Mine and the town's fabric—or, to be cliché, the space
between the two. We should build in and over and under the Open
Cut. It will just subside in entropy unless it is made urban.*
                              —the architect

I found you raw, cratered knee mapped
  with scar tissue   of the railroad track variety.
    You'd finished   with the one whose words
      I don't love you   *anymore* cleft you,
      and you'd left the   one who mined the neglect.
The topographical   change of Lead—1250 feet—
    breaks across a valley   and the Open Cut; the pit
    won't fill with water   as once imagined.
      What vision one   needs to design in spaces
    between, to bring   the open cut astronauts
    can spot from space   into conversation with
      the sloped streets   and picket fences of that
        mining village.   Your model features ghosted
          structures that   collapsed into Lead's maw.
      Her words, the next   one's guile, and my hand
        on your thigh exist   simultaneously. My project
        builds in and over and   under. No one had ever kissed
            the skin the oncologist stitched so close to the bone.
          We work because we question in love. Fingers against
                cheek, it leads where it leads;
                    we make it urban.

Ring Three

Every Day: We Live, Dream, Build

Everything is awesome when you're living the dream.
—lyrics from a *LEGO Movie* song

By the time we met, we'd already dumped
some hefty dreams. Divorce does that.
But living the dream—however ridiculous—
is so subtly seductive, just like Jefferson's grid
corrupted into cul-de-sacs meant to keep
the riffraff out, although no one admits
that motive for design. You say sustainability

is claptrap. From scratch it takes more energy
to build. What's better? Using the material
one has—remodeling, augmenting, considering
context, relationships. It's about the big picture.
Make it metropolitan. So here we are, a dream
team, and each day we stick brick to brick,

bread to bread, bed to bed. Each day we stack
snack on snack, book on book. Each day we stay
and build with what we have: two mini-figures—
children—one brown-haired, one blond; seizure
bricks, autism bricks, turbo bricks, trickster
bricks, peacemaker bricks, extrovert bricks—
energy, energy, energy—each morning back

to the LEGO table you built in a day to re-think,
add more, subtract time, try again. In the work
we find our way: clear a path, walk the edge,
push back peripheries, identify a corner, collect
a history, and voila! A building. Consider this
house, these four hearts—space as invention.

Acclimatize

The passive house—the home my husband
and I watched from skeleton
of board and steel to walls thick
with insulation, the house our son
thinks is ours because he kicked up
sawdust running along its planks—
features a homogenous
interior temperature,
sustainable despite winter's
negative forty-degree days.

In our skin's cells, intrinsic
heat works from a brush of a hand,
an ode to staircase, or a photo
of a well-worn dwelling. And when sundogs
appear, they glitter against the gauze
of sunrise, and I recall the morning
my husband arrived with snow frozen
in his hair, icicled eyelashes melting
from my touch. He helps build for balance;

our son, however, is a creature
of the cold. On nights the wind chill vacuums
breath, our preschooler spins stories
of ice railroads and woolly mammoths.
Yet after a full day of sledding
and sipping on snow-cones, he slipped into
our bed, between us, for warmth. He's
the reason I know that cold shifts
DNA. Relationship or
house—we design for heat.

Excess Rex

Our youngest son fears wildfires
and typhoons. He doesn't chatter
about the Prairie School style
gas station we scrutinized
on vacation, but he asks about
the blaze described on the plaque
across the street. I tell him the fire
happened years ago, yet in
nightmares embers land on his back.
He selects books: *What Makes
a Volcano?* and *The Ice Age Explained.*
One snowflake means blizzard. I heard
the radio; an ice storm's on
the way, he whispers, watching the window.

Months before his birth, his dad
texted the name: xavier rex.
He liked the visual anchor of x;
its meaning, *the new house*, persuaded
me to agree. We didn't know how
to say it. Now this blond, blue-eyed
boy pronounces his own story:
he hatched from an egg in Antarctica,
his igloo caught fire. Does he sense
the convergence that caused his conception
despite his parents' old age? Does he intuit
that serendipity delivered him
healthy and whole? A body that dreams
sparks sees no distinction between
extremes. For the new house, everything's
possible.

Playtime

With LEGOs, our son must play
your way. No rules, just free style.
Stack brick on brick on brick, you say.
With LEGOs, our son must play
and the first day, he doesn't disobey
your dictum. He submits to the trial.
With LEGOs, our son must play
your way: No rules, just free style.

When I build with him, I prefer
directions. Which LEGO goes where
on this set? I give the brick pile a stir.
When I build with him, I prefer
to study first and then refer
to the plan—no detour. I lack flair.
When I build with him, I prefer
directions; which LEGO goes where?

Our son's building style transcends ours.
He starts with an image, then innovates
with a variety of bricks for hours.
Our son's building style transcends ours:
car-room hybrids, boxes with gears. He scours
the brickpit as he links, builds, creates.
Our son's building style transcends ours;
he starts with an image, then innovates.

Four-Square

1.

I dream houses: a ghost-town bungalow
with stained glass that Tiffany would admire,
a gabled shotgun, a garden-encrusted chateau;
my sleep holds disorder and desire.

Most are dwellings I could never acquire:
a loft with vaulted ceilings, a condo
tucked into a skyscraper's elbow, a fire-
singed colonial with a castle-sized gazebo.

Then my grandparents' homes grow
from tiny spaces retirement required
into storied mansions. A scenario
my sleep holds: disorder of desire.

2.

In 1970, my grandparents sold
their modest brick and bought a mobile home
for travel money. They're fragile and bold,
our dreams to prosper and roam.

They kept it up: manicured lawn, garden gnome,
window planters. Retirees rolled
past in shiny Chryslers and sun-kissed comb-
overs. After grandpa died, my mom found mold-

covered walls in the trailer. She told
me they caused his mystery syndrome,
his death, that those flimsy walls were old.
So, too, our dreams to prosper and roam.

3.

Grandpa marked wood and sawed the thick
slabs, nailed them together and applied paint:
sunset blue. Dad lugged it home without a nick.
I'd dreamed of a doll house, cute and quaint,

to call my own. With money a constraint,
Mom knitted carpet for the floors—a sick
pea-green color. I didn't file a complaint,
nor did I make a mini home. Heartsick,

I sat my Barbie inside with a LEGO brick
for a book. And she exercised no restraint;
kid and kitchen-free, she read double-quick.
I'd dreamed of a doll house, cute and quaint.

4.

My sons want to assemble a gingerbread
house with frosting-glue, a candied roof,
green sugared windows—the snow dyed red.
Directions should make houses foolproof,

I think. The boys lick icing from walls and goof
up their order. They swallow gumdrops instead
of using them for décor. They unroof
the one standing and take a bite. Go ahead,

I say, as I spread
a door with snowflake sprinkles to spoof
what's on the box. Soon, we're all well-fed.
Directions don't make houses foolproof.

Divining the Layers

—after Pauline Aitken's *Strata*

Lamina, the name for sedimentary rock thin as paper,
paper similar to the sheets of my husband's sketches,
  sketches of façades and walls and interior spaces,
   spaces demarked by gradations, levels, or layers,
    layers similar to those found in the tissue of plants—
     plants with dermal, ground and vascular strata:
      strata of bodies—heart, skin, and blood cells,
       cells communicating or not—the unordering neurons,
        neurons in my son's brain underneath skin and skull,
         skull cupping labyrinth of fatty acids where cells fire,
          fire into subclinical seizures, data we capture and print,
           print on paper or study under microscopes or paint,
            paint in a rainbow of colors on a surface thin as lamina.

Architecture of His Brain

During sleep, the hippocampus and
   neocortex take part in a
      choreographed dialogue.

Brain folds embrace the seahorse-shaped
   formation as it unspools. To the beat,
      dendrites pulse. The dance begins.

Axons wave their arms as the day
   replays in a time-compressed capoeira—
      those impressions processed and stored.

Soon after slumber, my oldest son's
   brain boogies, but when the tempo
      shifts, spikes puncture his slow-wave

sleep and bust up the dance floor, some
   memories crowd-surfing
      into total oblivion;

others get stomped to bits in the mosh pit.
   Memories become wallflowers
      when neuron connection changes halt.

After he wakes with the club emptied,
   a photograph can coax a wallflower
      back to the dance floor where years-old

recollections of roller coasters
   and ocean waves can be labeled
      and stored as *happened yesterday*;

fireworks, carousel
  and full moon from last July
    tagged in the cache called *today*.

Fragmented steps, a few bars:
  he presents a new disco-
    dialogue for us to decipher.

Site Planning

—after Pauline Aitken's *Dendron*

As I cross this network of interstates
driving toward home, I'm dried out
of words until I hear *neural network*
on the radio, and I picture a lake
with streams that branch and taper.
Net. Work. My mother-made nets
for my oldest son: family, stories,
photos, arms reaching, reaching.
Across chasms, I've woven lifelines
to schools, doctors, and specialists
so he won't fall through. And as I drive
past fields so flooded I can't see
where they thin or end, I recall
the pervasiveness of his seizures—
one per minute when he slept.
They're receding now, but what
will they leave when they've dried up?
Some say new knowledge and new
memories; I imagine sunflower fields.
What work will my nets do then?
Perhaps he'll make his own trawls
weave into mine. Either way, each day
brings a facet of him to the surface,
polished and gleaming.

Anatomy

We need a new home with good bones,
he said. That first winter, he scanned
every surface with a laser.
Now a surgeon with a keyboard

and mouse, he dissects the model.
We've got a home with good bones,
and I see them as he slices
one way, hallways musculature

and stairs, arteries. Two more
clicks reveal organs: couch, chair, bed.
Our hundred-year-home with good bones
looks like a doll's house with its front

sheared-off, but its dolls aren't home, no
pixelated ghosts either, just
sheer pools of color: toy, blanket.
We're lungs in a home with good bones,

and outside the umbrella spines
of old trees hover as we breathe.

Love and Fear in a Pandemic

1.

Once, when pregnant with death, heart stopped
within my womb, I realized I loved
someone I'd never meet. I draw on that
vibration as April deepens in this
rural place, folks still lifting their laughter
to the sky in large, loquacious groups.
Last night, my husband said if he takes sick
and succumbs, he'll die thinking of me, and I
realized the power of loving through time.
Elsewhere, bodies pile up, hospitals
overwhelmed, and survivors grieve.
Despite the ache and anchor of these four walls,
during the quarantine, the quarantine,
I recall love, and for now, I stay in.

2.

If not in quarantine, I wouldn't think
twice about biking through a graveyard
and pausing at the Gerber daisies strewn
across loose soil, and I wouldn't wonder if
the 90-year-old died alone—nursing
home locked down—or surrounded by family.
If not in quarantine, I wouldn't raise
an eyebrow when my four-year-old asks
if we can bike through again to see
if a body's in an open pit,
and I wouldn't drop everything to find
a kid-friendly video on burials
only to have him throw his arms around

me when it's done: I hope you don't get the virus,
Mommy. If not in quarantine, my child
wouldn't worry this way.

3.
The pandemic puts pressure on love
and presents fear with a new playground.
Love's learning to teach our sons art,
math, reading; it's cooking three meals a day
and remote working under the microscope
of one another's gaze. Unmoored, we click
on graphs, charts, photos. Testimonies
of the sick, the dead, and the survivors
shape and story our fears. Metaphor falters
when we scrutinize the data, and we can't
find beauty there. Love's reaching for
each other only to find our scars relaxed.
Inside these walls, we have food, resources,
each other—love and fear's first real test.

Stress Warning

Chicago's forty-four story Big Red was finished
in 1972, but you didn't point it out on our tour.
Perhaps I missed its bright rust color due to days
of December rain-turned-snow, but most likely
it's because I just didn't know to look for
a rectangular, International Style icon in the skyline.

Did you know that in 1975, its windows began
to crack? Zigzagged fractures—a lightning storm
captured in glass. When I wonder out loud
about how architectural mistakes of that magnitude
occur, you tease me about never taking physics.
The motions of electrical charges and mechanical
behaviors that mystify me seem hard-wired in you,
but I do understand the tendency of matter

to change shape and area and volume in response
to heat and cold, cold, cold—just like my body,
your hands holding me and the days between.
I know it took you seven times to pass Calculus,
but it's possible to calculate for a snap. Even words
crack. Stress leaves such subtle lines on transparent
materials. Who remembers the person killed

when one pane of glass fell from the sky in 1999?
Not an architectural mistake—you say—that one's
on the engineers. I wonder if they regret not fixing
the problem before it got too late. Today, Big Red's
safe and strong on the Chicago skyline, the $18 million
retrofit appearing invisible, as prevention often does.

Summer of Smoke

We fought over fire as flames fed the smoke.
Later, you kissed me, and your lips shed the smoke.

Protests turn and cities burn. A dream deferred
explodes. Smothering justice will spread the smoke.

I savored roasted marshmallows and blistered
hot dogs. What I recall first instead? The smoke.

Tendril of milk in coffee; steam so thick it
scarfs my mouth. In everything, we read the smoke.

Flames transform blueprints and stories. My body's
a fire-vessel. A phoenix threads the smoke.

When fever architects my dreams, the song leaves
my city, music drops, and words wed the smoke.

Christine, you know ghost scents: bacon and bourbon,
rose and cigarettes. It's why you dread the smoke.

Ring Four

Trajectory Across Love's Long Axis

Swoon cycling, I spun and swirled
leaving spirals in my wake:

a nautilus, a thread curled.
Swoon cycling, I spun and swirled

on heart-charged feet. My steps whorled
wild: galaxy-shaped, a coiled snake.

Swoon cycling, I spun and swirled
leaving spirals in my wake.

Blueprints and Ghosts

My husband and I were midnight whispering
in the moment the soul opens after the body's
sated, that moment when everything's laid bare
and imagination, past, and present collide—
everything compossible—when he tells me
he helped design a project that still haunts him.

The clients? New Yorkers. Creepy, sleek, budget
unlimited. The elder, founder of the lingerie
store housed in every American mall, introduced
the younger client to the team, and he requested
a cabin, a picnic place for models featuring baskets,
bearskin rugs, and a fireplace for cold desert nights.

A glass wall overlooked a vista in New Mexico;
the road-facing wall was windowless save a few
narrow slits. Silk against skin. They shook hands.

How close can one get to evil before it tarnishes?
My husband's heart skittered across history: architects
who designed concentration camps and gallows.

He wondered how much they knew and when
and how they felt about knowing. He wondered
if design could help men to do bad better. At 55,
he can draw that cabin from memory—the same one
he drew at age 32, the year his daughter was born,
the year a surgeon scraped out a tumor from his knee—
and he can still feel that post-meeting handshake.
That cabin made the news this week: Predator. Sex

trafficking. Hundreds of girls. Now nightmares cross
my husband's midnights: his hand erases walls, line
after line, page after page until, as he rubs the last angle
away, the cabin returns. Over and over, he begins again.

Scopophilia

White
Rain is
a partial
nude—the place where
back, butt, and thigh meet
and hint female. This segment
fills the canvas, torso bent
and folded over
an outstretched leg,
dimpled back
bare and
white.

Art
compels
words which leave
my lips but fade
into the scrim our
playful theory talk
weaves. My gaze funnels. We walk
closer, my vision's
scope revising—
desire
becomes
art.

Look,
he says;
his collage
of insight lights
up our talk. Language
kaleidoscopes—all color
coded by quoted scholars:
the body passes
through space as we
look. As we
look, we
look.

Betwixt

For me, the space between is creamy
and supple, so much conceivable
between rounded Os and tailed Qs,
the possibilities between *hypotenuse*
and *hypnotic* endless. In poems,
space between lines is an accident
of sound or a guillotine of meaning.
Even forms and fonts can splice
and cleave slippery combinations.

My husband architects in liminal
spaces, in blur, in perception's
bounty. We peer through a gate
of Berlin's Old Jewish Cemetery,
where ivy greens graves and light
passes through a canopy of lindens
and chestnuts, illuminating gaps.
He lectures about Jews mourning,
conscripted German boys hanged
from trees, tombstones-turned-bullet
shields; I wonder about the space
between *scapegoat* and *scarlet*,
about definition and etymology,
about this thin slice of land
bearing witness to so much loss.

As we leave, my husband designs
for potential. For the Judengang's
processional path, he conjectures:
why not a John Hejduk archive?
a landing for viewing the graves?

a monument to murdered Jews?
My dictionary opens to *innocence*,
page mate to *innuendo*, words
I link for dimension and weight,
but the words I plumb and stretch?
Remember and *revision*,
requiem and *request*.

Research

My husband pours over aerial photographs
of land to the east of our South Dakota home.

Berms in the farmland, clusters of trees, faint
lines through crops help him trace a railroad line

long abandoned. He zooms to street view
and identifies caissons once used to support bridges.

They're crumbling, nearly obscured with grasses
and trees. He might drive there to collect

the taste of dust in his mouth. When he's gathered
enough evidence, he digs around archives: ads,

maps, photographs—anything to recreate a history
lost in the landscape. We both search this way,

moments of discovery and loss juxtaposed until
it transforms. I sift through memories, hold one up

to the light and replay it over and over and slow.
I consider all its facets, its tensions. Sometimes

art amplifies or crystallizes emotion; sometimes
the body makes meaning for itself. No matter

what the evidence, we counter the fading
effects of time as our disciplines whisper:

Tell where you've been,
               and we'll know where you'll go.

Marker of Medary

—first Dakota Territory town

As you photograph the monument,
story collapsed into bricks, know this:
after I die, it's you I'll haunt

fitfully, just as the time you've spent
studying this ghost town's genesis.
As you research the monument

and trace the founders' movement
away, sort Medary's history from artifice;
after a town dies, it's us it'll haunt.

Absence blots connections—the scent
of prairie memory too easy to dismiss.
As you model the monument

and scaffold your argument,
remember the horizon's analysis;
after a story dies, it's us it'll haunt.

Recall cultures we still misrepresent
and make your work a living interstice
as you redesign the monument.
After truth dies, it's the living it'll haunt.

Mall Manifesto

My husband loves to hate malls, loves
to trash talk the capitalist cookie cutters:
Everyone's buying the same pants from GAP!
He ducks in and buys five pair. His home mall?
NorthPark, Dallas, its one million white bricks
highlighting the clean, modern lines he adores.
During our visit, we missed the works of Andy
Warhol and Frank Stella in its art gallery,
but we strolled past Mark di Suvero's *Ad Astra*,
orange steel I-beams heavy in the airy place.
When we watch *True Stories* (1986), my husband
loves to point out the store where he bought
his first wife's engagement ring when characters
walk by. Store's not there anymore, he notes.

As teens, my friends and I—suburban mall rats—
loved to roam Merle Hay Mall, loved to dart
between shoppers in pursuit of cute boys
and duck into Spencer's silicone scents
and incense, mesmerized by punkish t-shirts,
amused by innuendoes. In our spiked bangs
and stirrup pants, we roved that Iowa mall,
coveting $250 sweaters at Benneton and jeans
at The Limited even though we had to scrape
together babysitting money to buy a pizza.
The only art I remember—besides the chiseled
quarterbacks or corn-fed wrestlers we spied on—
were the framing gallery's posters of the Patrick
Nagel variety. Now with two of its four anchors
empty, I ask my husband to re-imagine the space.
Why not housing for the elderly? he replies.

There's not much to love or to hate about
the mall in Watertown, South Dakota—
the one closest to our home. In the mornings,
mall walkers keep tight to the perimeter before
store gates are raised, before high-heeled
ladies and teens in khakis turn on screens,
thirsty for morning sales. Walkers converse,
voices bouncing off walls and filtering through
"La Bamba" and "Rockin' Robin."
Perhaps they recall when malls buzzed, every box
filled, fast food joints sending fried aromas into
Walden's, Sears, Zales. The liver of a town's body—
malls as cleansing commerce. They were teens
when Victor Gruen designed the mall as a modern
forum, as an agora. Malls were new town squares
by the time they could push their kids through
air-conditioned sweetness in their strollers.

I want to love this mall as I loved Merle Hay,
as my husband loves a good building. I want
to love its studios of regional artists and its spaces
for local shops; I want to crave the nachos
served at Señor Max's, but the energy's not here.
Mall walkers bid each other goodbye in front
of a store directory, half its names blacked out.
Wall displays are vacant, dated, or dusty. I wonder
if my husband and I will be walkers someday.
While waiting for him to get the car, I'll hang
back on a bench, too, as one woman does, hand
on my purse, the struggling stores hungry for
what's inside it. If my husband has taught me
anything, it's that good design can promote
the intellectual, emotional, and physical
work of the people who use a space.

What happens when the money's gone,
spent in other ways? Maybe, in twenty years,
malls will house grocery stores and libraries,
preschools and office spaces. Maybe, in twenty
years, a mall won't be a mall at all.

A Good Building

In South Dakota, we've got good soil.
Mineral-rich. Enough moisture. It filters,
the soil here. It's soaked up spilled blood—
not spilled like milk or tea—lives were ended.
I mean families were murdered. I mean
whole communities were disappeared.
Disease. Deprivation. I mean to stop
using passive voice.

In the 1930s, Professor Ralph Patty
exemplified three ancient architectural
processes to make poultry barns
on our campus: wood, concrete,
and rammed earth—made like it sounds.
Soil composition and thermodynamics
means only the rammed earth work
still stands. And the 30s? That was only
sixty years after this space was cleared,
I mean colonized; only sixty years after
this place was pioneered, peopled, opened up—
I mean to stop using euphemisms.
I mean genocide. I mean holocaust.

Not like Germany's exactly. But when
I walked into Berlin's Chapel of Reconciliation
built on the once deadly no man's land,
the temperature changed. Its layers
of rammed earth are composed of pressed ash,
clay, and material from the former church
on that site. I felt the energy in those walls,

the energy in that earth. I mean that without
candles and pews and icons and stained glass
it felt sacred.

Rammed earth. It must be proposed,
muscled, pressed, treated. It must
be engaged, not owned. Soil that's part
of actual land. Even the Greeks, arbiters
of reason and logic, recognized synecdoche's
power: the part represents the whole.

Professors of architecture modeled
a rammed earth wall for our campus's
new American Indian Student Center
composed of earth from South Dakota's
Cheyenne River, Crow Creek, Flandreau
Santee, Lower Brule, Pine Ridge, Rosebud,
Lake Traverse, and Standing Rock Reservations.
I mean it was planned. I mean there were
lean years. I mean there were budget cuts.
Now the façade will be the usual
brick—painted to appear like earth.

Composite City: A Cento

In this half-embrace of earth, this pelvic
        amphitheater of the Mother, sunk in a bowl
   of sky trimmed with marbled statuary
          (slate, snow, ash)—a dazed array
              dipped in the moon's cold palette.

      Told not to, I stalked the city anyway—
ziggurat of steel, zeitgeist of bread
          and 2000 cheeses. Cattails sharp and silver
      in the first light vied with the steeples, knives
and scissors all out there. The courtyard
          and walls are yellow stone, as if a jinn
      poured sun into sand and hardened it.

The city growls like a hunting tiger.

          I want to imagine the aerial map that will
     send me above flame trees, snaking through
            knots of basalt. Skeletal rooms outlined
        on the city plan refused to reveal their origins.
Traveling by bicycle rickshaw past silk shops
          is a thirst for moonlight that will solidify sun.

     Around me birch, pine, concrete block houses
          rose from razed landscape. Grove of steel pillars.
      The leftover edifice of empire sprouts trees.

A bus window framed the appeared city,
             structure suggested by checks of chinks
     dissolving in smoke. Dried-up leaves,
       skidding like iceboats on their points down

winter streets. I hear the temple gong,
summoning the faithful, and in the lull of echo,
the jangle of bells on the women's ankles.

The city wakes with a song upon her mouth.

Retiro, they say, is the city's one lung.
The trolley car stopped in its slot seals
itself again and becomes a terrarium
for plants in sweaters and topcoats. Steel
rails gleam with fatigued light. Wheels
and rails in their prime collide, make love
in glide of slickness and friction. Life hums,
a wire pulled taut between
that street and one across an ocean.

Frescoes falling into piles of blue
and gold. I can't climb that staircase
leading nowhere, rising from debris,
and behave as if stone walls were no
different than souls. A woman in sparkling
green stands among antennas and satellite
dishes, hanging laundry on an invisible line.

Elemental Lesson

> *He who seeks truth shall find beauty.*
> —Moshe Safdie

When my husband said brutalist,
I thought oppressive and impenetrable
because I lacked imagination.
In Montréal, we biked by *Habitat 67*
and the one-hundred forty-six
block-stacked apartments emerged
from the shadowless landscape—sky
and cubes gray upon gray, all
concrete and corner with rectangle
windows wrapping the tops. He pointed
out stairs, access points, garden spots.

When he said brutalist and concrete,
I thought severe and unevolved because
mixing limestone, gravel, sand, and cement
meant rough and simple, like sidewalks.
In Collegeville, Minnesota, we drove
toward St. John's Abbey, concrete
curved across blue sky, an undulation
stilled. Cast into wooden frames on site,
the church looked like folds of fabric.
Inside: a symphony of stained glass
and honeycomb windows, sunlight
the texture of tulle. In that space,
where Marcel Breuer designed every
element to seek truth, my understanding
transfigured. Light stands for God
in that place concrete created.

Map and Meaning

For years, I waited for a map
as if anticipating a savior.
I wanted it to tell me what mattered
most. To practice divining, I traced
concentric elevation lines,
splotches of lakes, and curving rivers
on maps of others. I ciphered climate
and topography, reservoirs
and resources, roads and dead
ends. On globes, I touched the smooth
Atlantic and raised Himalayas,
but outdated ones disturbed me.
How could a country change its borders?
Shed its name? Disappear?

A few times, I sketched out
a neighborhood. Others outlined
interstate systems and beltways,
inked-in rivers and island cities.
Once someone who claimed to love
me painted a perimeter.
It's tough to make one's own map.
I predicted my true map would be
unconventional: turquoise mass
like a broken Pangaea, corners
smudged gold, orange oval
and gray-hued rings hovering.
My map marked the spiral of stops
along my path. In its abstraction,
my map made everything mean.

Credo

Fractal: a cascade of never-ending, self-similar, repeated elements that change in scale but retain similar shape.

A
cascade
of
infinite
is why
I believe in
loops
and spirals,
subtle shifts, cycles.
My son,
preschooler stunned
by
the science museum,
sticks his hand
into a glacier,
the chunk
a broken testimony,
the history
of
a world dissolving. *Cold!*
It's cold! And
it's melting. Look right here, he says.
Similarities
of self
astonish. I see them in
architecture,
geometry a welcome language,
shapes
a new alphabet for

prayer and song.

I study Peter Eisenman's

House 11a

lapping up patterns, interlocking Ls,

squares and

replicated rectangles—

the syntax of

ideas. For Frank Gehry's Guggenheim

in

Bilbao, syntax looks like

titanium scales rhyming across curves. Glass

and limestone

patterns, similarities of

visual texture,

are creations of weight, depth; order breaks

tension

where the lines turn. A cascade

of repeating elements grounds my belief in

humanity

as mystery. Signs appear: a sound,

song,

and syllable mean things.

Armadillo! Armadillo! sings my son,

the youngest,

using his Louis Armstrong

voice; grit gives way to twang and twang turns into hard-rock screams.

He's an oracle

at four years old, an armor-clad mammal

his muse.

My oldest son speaks in code,

echolalia a symptom of a seizure-

besieged brain. When

he utters, *No* and *No* and *No* and

No,

then *I don't know I don't know I don't know,* I listen for
a divine voice revealed.
Cascades changing in scale, not shape, is why I
trust weight, depth,
height—materials and thingness:
Saturn's rings, the Pacific coastline, bolts of lightning,
a Romanesco
cauliflower, angelica flower-
heads, veins
of sycamore leaves, seashells, snowflakes, blood vessels, DNA.
A range and scope of fractals
inspire awe, a cascade of never-ending
wonder at both
connections and aberrations as
well
as places of perfect order and broken patterns. When
I consider what we
may be reduced-sized copies of, I grapple
with insight;
it hovers in physics and biology, the shapes of letters,
the magic of new languages,
the mystery of cells and synapses, the music
of my sons' voices,
the geometries of buildings and trees.
Sometimes
I glimpse an answer, something like seeing starlight years after
the star dies, supernovas.
Four hours before my youngest son's birth, I dreamed
my sister, dead
31 years, placed him in my arms: *Take care of him,* she said. He has
her eyes, ice-blue and illumined by
God.

Acknowledgments

Grateful acknowledgment is made to the following journals in which some of the poems in this collection first appeared, sometimes with different titles:

Big Muddy: "A Good Building," "Every Day: We Live, Dream, Build"

Briar Cliff Review: "When You're Away, I Think About Form"

The Ekphrastic Review: "Divining the Layers"

Gatherings Project: "Love and Fear in a Pandemic"

Gyroscope Review: "Congruence"

Indian River Review: "Map and Meaning"

MacQueen's Quinterly: "Elemental Lesson," "Site Planning," "Summer of Smoke"

Midwest Review: "Palimpsest"

Mom Egg Review: "Excess Rex"

Natural Bridge: "Didactic"

New Plains Review: "All My Engineering"

North American Review: "Witch Loves Architect"

Pasque Petals: "Poet Prepares for Love," "Research"

Peauxdunque Review: "Brand: Bring Your Dreams"

Pilgrimage Magazine: "Betwixt," "Marker of Medary"

The Sheepshead Review: "Dimensional Shift"

South Dakota Magazine: "Medical Arts Building"

South Dakota Review: "An Architect's Blessing," "Love on a Grid," "Outlaw"

Terrain.org: "Anatomy," "Urban Planning"

The third stanza of "Love and Fear in a Pandemic" was reprinted in *The New York Times* on November 26, 2020.

"Medical Arts Building" was reprinted in *More in Time: A Tribute to Ted Kooser*, ed. Jessica Poli et al. (University of Nebraska Press, 2021).

I'd like to thank Diane Lockward for choosing my manuscript for Terrapin Books; I appreciate the work she does for poets, poems, and poetry lovers. Thanks to fellow poets who read these poems as drafts and offered valuable insight: Lysbeth Em Benkert, Rochelle Harris Cox, Barbara Duffey, Jeanne Emmons, Lindy Obach, Pen Pearson, Marcella Remund, Erika Saunders, and Norma C. Wilson. Thanks to South Dakota State University, South Dakota Art Museum, and the Rapid City Arts Council (Adelstein Art Grant) for gifts of time and financial support. Thanks to the South Dakota State Poetry Society for their dedication to the promotion of poetry across the state. And thanks to the many teachers, artists, architects, poets, and scholars whose work informed my own. Finally, with deep appreciation for my family, including my parents, who made space for me to write and provided loads of inspiration.

About the Author

Christine Stewart-Nuñez, South Dakota's poet laureate (2019-2023), is the author of four books of poetry, most recently *Untrussed* (University of New Mexico Press, 2016) and *Bluewords Greening* (Terrapin Books, 2016), winner of the 2018 Whirling Prize. In 2019, the South Dakota Council of Teachers of English named her Author of the Year. As a professor at South Dakota State University, Christine's teaching, creative work, and service have earned accolades, including the Dr. April Brooks Woman of Distinction Award (2020) and the Outstanding Experiential Learning Educator Award (2019). She served on the board of directors for the South Dakota State Poetry Society from 2012-2018 and edited its poetry magazine, *Pasque Petals*, from 2014-2018. She's the founder of the Women Poets Collective, a regional group focused on advancing their writing through peer critique and support. She lives in Brookings with her husband, Brian T. Rex, a professor of architecture, and her two sons.

christinestewartnunez.com

CPSIA information can be obtained
at www.ICGtesting.com
Printed in the USA
BVHW031324230621
610212BV00005B/435

9 781947 896451